THINGS
KIDS
COLLECT!

Other Books by Shari Lewis

THINGS KIDS COLLECT!

How to Become a Successful
Treasure Hunter

by
Shari Lewis

Leo Behnke, consultant
Illustrations by Helen McCarthy
Art Direction by John Brogna

Holt, Rinehart and Winston
New York

Library of Congress Cataloging in Publication Data

Lewis, Shari.
    Things Kids Collect.

(Kids-Only Club)
Includes index.
SUMMARY: Suggests activities for collectors interested in more than 25 different collectibles such as rocks, keys, buttons, and menus.
1. Collectors and collecting — Juvenile literature.
[1. Collectors and collecting.   2. Hobbies]
I. McCarthy, Helen.   II. Title.
AM231.L48   790.1'32   79-3838
ISBN 0-03-049731-0
ISBN 0-03-049736-1 (pbk.)

Printed in the United States of America
10   9   8   7   6   5   4   3   2   1

Dedication

To the happy memory of my in-laws, Jack and Mary Tarcher, who collected beautiful things and taught their fine son to enjoy all the beauty the world has to offer.

Acknowledgments

Dear Kyle Husfloen, *Antique Trader Weekly*; Mary E. Croker, *Hobbies* Magazine, *Collectors' News* (dolls); United Federation of Dolls Club (dolls); Judy Phillips, NFL Properties, Inc. (sports pennants / patches); Gene Parill, Marque Products (scale model cars); Edward Kapitanoff, ELK Enterprises, Inc. (scale model cars); Irv Desfor (photography); Tony Hyman (boxes); Tidepool Gallery (shells); Abner Kreisberg Coin Gallery (coins); American Numismatic Association (coins); Minkus Stamp & Publishing Co. (stamps); James Magruder III (stamps); Van Dahl Publications (stamps); Sy Ziv, Toys-R-Us (toys); Scott Suieback, Toy Mart of Beverly Hills (miniatures/toys); Vince Alati (toys); Jim Carrigan, J.C. Penney Co., Inc. (toys/miniatures); David Benjamin, (sports cards); Cory Cooper, (stickers); The Rendells, Inc. (autographs); Don Coney, Joseph Hayes, American Political Item Collectors (buttons/badges); Charles Chandler, American Lock Collectors Assn. (keys); Malcolm Willits, Collectors Book Store (books); Allen Cook (puppets); Mrs. Rillis Heady Pacific Shell Club (shells); Ray Avery, Avery's Rare Records (records); WRC Shedenhelm, *Rock and Gem* Magazine (rocks); Sgt. Pierce Weir (Great Western Boy Scout Council); Paula Caputo (troop leader, Angeles Girl Scout Council); Rori Lindo, Sydney Turk and Hank Schulman (additional research with young people):

This is just a wee note to thank you for sharing your fine expertise with my research staff and me as we put together *Things Kids Collect*.

We're very grateful to all of you. If you ever need any advice on communications between animals and people, Lambchop and I are at your service!

Love,

Shari Lewis

Contents

Shawn

FOTO
FUN

Barker

Jimmy

Georgia

Mally

Twerp

8

Introduction

Lots of kids start collections without half trying. They put together whole bunches of keys, or shelves full of dolls, or enough stickers to cover every notebook in the entire school!

But often kids don't know what's worth saving and what isn't, where to look for more, what to do with all the stuff once they've got it, and who to turn to for answers to all their questions.

That's what *Things Kids Collect* is all about—a peek at 27 different things that make good collectibles, and ideas on the best ways to handle these treasures.

We interviewed over 1,000 young people in summer camps on the East coast, schools and playgrounds in the West, and even 50 kids waiting in line to get into the *Muppet Movie*. As they shared their interests, they not only gave us answers, but lots of "would-be" collectors in the groups asked questions like:

Why do people want to collect stuff?

For some, collecting combines the excitement of a treasure hunt with the fun of owning things that you like. Someone said, "This is another way of hunting. You can't really go into the woods with a bow and arrow anymore, but you *can* hunt for things you love. And the hunting for *just* what you want is more important than *having* that thing and putting it on your shelf."

Most objects that used to be made of metals and glass and other expensive materials are now created out of plastic. As many years go by and fine old objects become rare, they're worth more and more. (Toy tin soldiers that sold for $1.00 a set 5 or 10 years ago often sell at auctions today for almost $100.)

Many collectors buy stuff at one price, hold it for a few years, and sell it at a higher price. They make money while doing what they like to do best.

What do people collect?

Almost anything!

Some grownups specialize in things they can *use* — like Tiffany lamps, watches and clocks, furniture, or antique cars. Others spend fortunes on things like gemstones or rare paintings. Then there are lots of adults who love to lay their hands on funny funky things, like bumper stickers, beer cans, bottle caps, or barbed wire. (Yes, barbed wire!)

For *Things Kids Collect*, I've had to pick and choose. For instance, I left out piggy banks, bells, and balls. Some "packrats" *do* collect those, but I had to stop *somewhere*!

Where do I look?

First, find out if family and friends have what you're searching for, tucked away in attics and cellars. Next, make regular trips to garage sales, swap meets, flea markets, Salvation Army and Goodwill stores, and other thrift shops. This kind of source is really cheaper than a store that sells *only* a certain object (like a rock shop or toy store). Every once in a while, you'll uncover a humdinger that will make all the scrounging around worthwhile.

If you live in a big city, look for your treasure as you travel. Prices are often lower in small towns. And don't be afraid to offer less money than it says on the price tag. That's called bargaining or haggling, and it's a good way for a collector to beat the asking price.

How do I find out more about my hobby?

Ask! Turn to older friends who share your interst. Get to know storekeepers and business people around you. (For example, a printer might be able to help you with your menu collection, while a person who buys and sells with foreign countries might have stamps for you.)

Books are gold mines of facts and fun. Your librarian will be more than happy to help you put your hands on a book that will tell you what you want to know.

Make trips to museums and visit special exhibits of

dolls, miniatures, costumes, or whatever you fancy. You'll see new things you might not know about and great ways to organize your collection.

Do I have to organize my collection? Can't I just collect?

From the very start, it's a good idea to sort your stuff, so that things that are alike are kept together (say, shells lined up on a shelf according to *size*, or by *family* — whichever pleases you).

The reason for this is simple. Before you know it, you'll probably have a whole lot of whatever you choose to collect. If you can lay your hands on the one thing you want when you want it, you'll get much more pleasure out of your hobby. Others will be impressed, too, and will respect what you're doing.

A super way to organize your collection is to have a 3 × 5 card for *each piece*. On it, put the name of the article, when and where you got it, from whom, how much it cost, and where it can be found within your collection.

How do I find others who have the same interest?

As soon as you can, join a club—even if it's a national club and you never get to meet the other members in person. Belonging to a club will help you find out more about the things you collect. Most clubs have a newsletter or magazine which will give you lots of fascinating information.

Your library probably has a book called the *Encyclopedia of Associations*. It lists 100 groups, and by writing to the national organization that interests you, you can find out whether there's a club in your neighborhood.

The Kids-Only Club gang — Shawn, Mally, Georgia, Jimmy, Twerp, and Barker—and I have found that kids with hobbies lead more interesting lives. If you have a hobby, you find out what you like, and it helps you to know who you are.

I hope that somewhere in *Things Kids Collect*, you'll find some that will make a "packrat" out of *you*.

Anything /
Everything

IT'S UP TO YOU

Some people collect anything and everything they can find about the things that interest them most.

I know a girl who loves horses. Her room is full of horse statues, calendars, pillows, photographs, windup toys, keychains, books—in other words, anything she can get her hands on in the shape of a horse, or about a horse.

Then there are kids who are car-crazy. Some hunt for stuff about one particular car, say a jeep. Others round up models, brochures, mechanical toys and what-have-you relating to any old car!

There are science fiction buffs who are always on the lookout for *Star Wars* or *Star Trek* materials—or both.

You can do the same. Pick a subject or object that makes you feel good. Collect whatever you can about it. Pretty soon, your family and friends will start searching out items for you, too. They'll *like* doing this because now they know exactly what to give you for Christmas and birthdays. So, pass the word—

GETTING IT TOGETHER

Whether your love is cats or monsters, you'll like being surrounded by your treasures. Keep as much of your collection as you can out on display. Small figures can go on your desk, night table, or shelves; pictures, on the wall.

If you put your goodies into boxes, label them on the outside so you won't have to open the box to find out what's in it. Groups of small boxes can go into larger boxes which can be slid under your bed.

13

Try to keep *related* things together as much as possible. For instance, if you collect tiny little animals of all kinds, you can either keep the monkeys in one spot and the bears in another—or you can separate all of the china figures from the glass ones.

If there's more than one item in a box, use a separator or padding so they won't bump together.

Store paper items in file folders. They'll last longer and stay flat.

GOOD, BETTER, BEST

Because this kind of collecting is so much a part of you, what's *best* is what pleases *you* the most. As you collect, look for one-of-a-kind items that you don't already own. If you have more than one, trade with friends and get something that your collection is missing. As you go along, try to get the *best* you can.

HELP! AND MORE HELP—

Old Things for Young People by Ann K. Cole; David McKay Co., New York.

Collector's News, Box 156, Grundy Center, Iowa 50638.

Hobbies Magazine, 1006 South Michigan Avenue, Chicago, Illinois 60605.

Advertising/ Souvenirs

IT'S UP TO YOU

An advertising collection can include anything with a product or company's name or design on it: ashtrays, mirrors, trays, salt and pepper shakers, toys, puzzle sets, playing cards, bookmarks, calendars, newspaper and magazine ads, and giveaways of all sorts.

If the packages and ads you gather are from the 1870s to 1904, they're called antique advertising art.

Souvenirs can be pennants or buttons, dishes or spoons, jewelry or clothing, silly hats or postcards or anything else on which a city, state, amusement park, county fair, world's fair, or, say, ballclub, puts its name.

GETTING IT TOGETHER

The size and shape of the things you collect will determine the best way to keep your collection all together. If you collect bookmarks, you certainly won't need the

same box or shelf space that you would for novelty hats. Just try to protect your finds from dust, too much sunlight, and other damage. And *do* start a card file to help you keep track of each item in your collection.

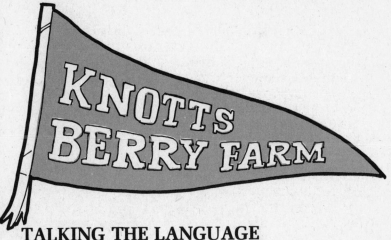

TALKING THE LANGUAGE

Here's some of the basic vocabulary that every advertising collector should know.

- Consumer—person who buys the product.
- Personalized—any item stamped or decorated with a person's name or initials.
- Premium—an object offered by an advertiser as a "special offer."
- Print media—newspapers and magazines used for advertising.
- Promotion — a particular advertising campaign, usually involving a one-time-only premium.
- Set—a group of related objects put out together (like a pack of sports trading cards).

HELP! AND MORE HELP—

Collector's News, Box 156, Grundy Center, Iowa 50638.

Autographs

IT'S UP TO YOU

Some autograph hounds try to dig up signatures of movie stars only — or of musicians, singers, artists, ballplayers, or even presidents of the United States!

Others try to keep a record of all the people who touch their *own* lives by collecting signatures from every teacher or best friend they have.

You could continue a school album begun by one of your parents, and add your own school chums as the years go by.

HOW TO START

You can get people's signatures by:

- Writing to them — (include a stamped self-addressed envelope).
- Meeting them—go to book stores for autographing parties (they're often given for science fiction authors and writers of children's books) or go to ball games and take along something special to be signed—a ball or the trading cards of the particular players in that game.
- Buying the autographs from dealers—they're listed in the telephone directory.

Carry a small supply of blank 3 × 5 cards with you wherever you go, together with a felt tip pen. If you're prepared, you'll never be in the awful position of meeting the person but missing the autograph.

GOOD, BETTER, BEST

Autographed pictures of TV and movie stars sent to you from the studios aren't generally worth any money. Sometimes they're not even signed by the star. If you collect 'em, just enjoy looking at them!

Old autographs in good condition and attached to letters or documents are more valuable.

Never tear a signature off the original sheet. An autograph is much more precious when it is signed on something—a memorandum, letter, note or even a laundry list—than it would be just by itself.

(In 1978, I was chairperson of the American Lung Association Christmas Seal campaign. Some sharp people around the country sent me sheets of the 1978 Christmas seals to sign, because their hobby was getting the autograph of each Lung Association Chairperson on the sheet of seals related to that person.)

Old autographs aren't *necessarily* valuable. It depends on how many copies of that signature are floating around and whether anyone else wants it. (George Washington's signature is worth less than President William Henry Harrison's, even though Washington's is older, and he was, of course, a more famous president. You see, Washington was said to have personally signed every letter during his two terms in office, while Harrison died only a month after he became president and thus signed very few.)

GETTING IT TOGETHER

Never paste anything into your albums. Use photomount corners. Autographs can be framed and hung on a wall, or filed in manila folders.

Each index card should list the name of the person who signed the autograph, the date when you got it, the price (if any), the person you got it from, the size and number of pages attached to the signature, and where it is located in your collection (so you can find it in a hurry).

THE COLLECTOR'S DREAM

One ambition is to find an unknown manuscript by a famous author with his or her signature on it. (This happened a few years ago when someone found a manuscript written by Edgar Allan Poe hidden in a secret drawer of a desk.)

Another great goal of autograph collectors is to find a genuine signature of William Shakespeare.

HELP! AND MORE HELP—

Autographs: A Key to Collecting by Mary A. Benjamin; Walter R. Benjamin, New York.

Fundamentals of Autograph Collecting by the Rendells; 154 Wells Avenue, Newton, Massachusetts 02159.

Universal Autograph Collectors Club, P. O. Box 467, Rockville Centre, New York 11571.

Automobilia

IT'S UP TO YOU

You can collect parts of cars (like license plates), information about cars (like owner's manuals, repair manuals or copies of the *Blue Book Used Car Price Guide* for each year). You might scratch around for advertising items used to sell cars (photographs, brochures or dealers' signs) or novelties either with emblems of car manufacturers on them or in the shape of cars (like keyrings). You can hunt for things that relate to one brand of auto, specialize in American or foreign made cars, or look for what-have-you from cars that are no longer being manufactured. Some people add authentic models of cars to their collection, and colored postcards of those antique cars now in museums and private collections.

WHERE TO LOOK

Car dealers are a good source of advertising materials, especially when the new cars have come in and the dealers are dumping stuff about last year's models. You can also check junkyards (look in the classified telephone directory), repair garages, and service stations. If there's a branch office of a car manufacturer nearby, contact the public relations office.

Parts of old cars are expensive at swap meets and when bought through ads in magazines, but if your family drives into the country, hunt through the junk shops you pass, and do explore the nooks and crannies of old barns.

THINGS YOU'LL NEED

If you collect hardware (for example, headlights or engine parts made of chrome, brass or stainless steel), you'll need some cleaners such as Formula 409, Bon Ami, alcohol, and Gumout. Metal polishes will be useful, as will glues and paints, for touching up here and there. A few tools will come in handy—for example, to tighten up screws on the mounting strap of a distributor, to replace parts, say, on a carburetor, or to fasten things together.

HELP! AND MORE HELP—

Floyd Clymer Publications, 222 No. Virgil Ave., Los Angeles, California 90004 specializes in automotive books and booklets. Send for their catalog.

Cars and Parts Magazine, Sesser, Illinois 62884.

There are too many auto magazines on newstands today to list them all here. Find one that interests you.

If you fancy cars, you'll want to visit car barns and museums. They exist in many parts of the country. Check your local office of the American Automobile Association for listings of local car museums, clubs, and collectors.

IT'S UP TO YOU

You might choose to collect books about a subject that interests you (like science fiction, the Civil War, or magic), or books about a person or country. You can go after a certain *kind* of book (fiction or nonfiction, historical biographies, children's books, books of photographs and so on).

Some hobbyists are on the lookout for every edition of a certain magazine or all issues of a magazine that came out in a particular year.

Other people try to track down comic books about a favorite character, or comics issued during a certain period (for example, the late '40s or early '50s).

WHERE TO LOOK

Ask friends, neighbors and relatives (especially older ones) for books, magazines and comics they no longer want. Go to garage sales, swap meets, thrift and second-hand stores, Goodwill, Salvation Army, and veterans association stores. Book dealers are excellent sources, especially when you need or want a specific item for your collection — but their prices will be higher than elsewhere.

THINGS YOU'LL NEED

Sandwich bags in two or three different sizes to protect your magazines and comics are a necessity. Get price guides and catalogs from book dealers so you'll know the going rates and what's available on your particular subject.

If possible, make a simple bookplate or label with

your name on it, so that you can mark each item as yours.

GETTING IT TOGETHER

Books and magazines look best on shelves, with the magazines lying flat, not standing up. They can be arranged alphabetically by subject, author, date (for historical subjects), countries, language, or however you choose.

Start an index file with each 3 × 5 card listing one book or magazine issue. Put the name of the author or editor, title, date when it was published, publisher, the date when you got it, the price you paid, and any other special scoop. This card file can be set up alphabetically by author's name, title, or subject.

GOOD, BETTER, BEST

Most magazines or comics are not worth much unless they are in mint condition. Here's how books, magazines, and comics are graded:

- Mint—like new, perfect, flat, and clean.
- Very fine—slight wear, still glossy.
- Fine—some wear, shiny but clean.
- Very good—minor wear, no gloss or shine, minor markings.
- Good—used, slightly soiled, some creases, minor tears.
- Fair—many wrinkles, soiled, slightly damaged.
- Poor—damaged, dirty.

THE COLLECTOR'S DREAM

In comic books, the collector strikes gold when he or she finds a copy of any comic book from the early 1960s or earlier in fine condition. The first issue of comic heroes like Superman, Wonder Woman, Batman, or Plasticman would be a genuine treasure.

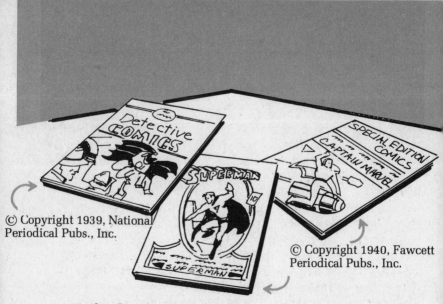

© Copyright 1939, National Periodical Pubs., Inc.

© Copyright 1940, Fawcett Periodical Pubs., Inc.

In books, the find would be a first edition with the original paper dust jacket, in mint condition, signed by the author to a famous friend—especially if it's the first copy of an edition of which very few copies were printed.

HELP! AND MORE HELP—

The Collector's Book of Books by Eric Quayle, Clarkson N. Potter, New York.

Collector's News, Box 156, Grundy Center, Iowa 50638, is a monthly which has a classified column with book and magazine ads.

American Book Price Current: ABPC, 121 East 78th Street, New York 10021 (for used book prices).

Overstreet Comic Book Price Guide; Robert Overstreet, Division of Crown, New York.

Bottles

IT'S UP TO YOU

Bottles come in lots of sizes, shapes, and colors. In fact, it's amazing how many different kinds of glass containers there are: medicine and milk bottles, syrup and flavors bottles, soda pop, wine and liquor bottles, fruit jars, ink bottles, and miniatures of all kinds.

You can concentrate on cosmetic bottles and jars (Avon Products are very big with collectors), bottles in special shapes or with pictures on them, and even glass and ceramic insulators from electric power poles.

Some folks try to locate bottles made and marked in certain parts of the country. For example, old ink bottles are often stamped with the name of the city where they were made.

Bitters bottles are popular because the little containers are so wonderfully shaped. Some are like a fish, others like a tiny bunch of grapes, still others, square.

WHERE TO LOOK

Start with your relatives. Perhaps your grandparents or an aunt has an old bottle collection you can start with.

Every once in a while, check out your local dump, or even places where people aren't *supposed* to dump things, but do. Any open land where buildings used to stand is a good place to dig (get the owner's permission, of course). The desert is a good source — not because there are a lot of bottles but because the ones you *do* find will probably be rather old and may have turned an unusual color from having been out in the sun. Skin-diving in lakes and the ocean will also turn up a wide variety of glass jars and jugs.

THINGS YOU'LL NEED

Containers that have paper labels shouldn't be washed. Those labels are important because they tell so much about the bottle. Use brushes with stiff bristles to clean off dirt. A good magnifying glass will help you to check mold marks and small print on bottles and labels.

TALKING THE LANGUAGE

- Captain's decanter—a squat bottle with large, flat bottom (sometimes called a ship's decanter).
- Figural—a container in the shape of a person or animal (like the Mrs. Butterworth Pancake Syrup bottle or some of the containers put out by Avon).
- Milk glass—white opaque glass (that means light

can pass through the glass, but you can't *see* through it).

- Mold mark—a line around any molded glass object showing where the two parts of the mold came together.
- Seal—an extra piece of glass or special wax attached to the side of a bottle, found on old bottles and on new ones that are made to *look* old.

GOOD, BETTER, BEST

Bottle collecting values depend on the age, condition, and rarity of each container. In some cases, the color also makes a difference (if, for example, most others of a particular type of jar are a different color).

A bottle with no mold marks is generally over 100 years old.

Each Coca-Cola bottle used to have the name of the city where it was made imprinted on the bottom. If you come across one of these, you'll know you have an oldie.

HELP! AND MORE HELP—

Illustrated Guide to Collecting Bottles by Cecil Munsey; Hawthorn Books, New York.

Kovel's Complete Bottle Price List by Ralph and Terry Kovel; Crown Publishers, New York.

The Book of Bottle Collecting by Doreen Beck; Hamlyn Ltd., London.

Hobbies Magazine, 1006 South Michigan Avenue, Chicago, Illinois 60605.

Old Bottle Magazine,. Box 243, Bend, Oregon, 97701.

Milkbottles Only Organization (MOO), 305 East Oxford Street, Alexandria, Virginia 22301.

Boxes

IT'S UP TO YOU

There are plastic boxes of all sizes and colors, wooden boxes, leather boxes, little metal pillboxes, boxes in the shape of miniature luggage or animals, as well as boxes made out of seashells or covered with lacquered paper. You can concentrate on boxes that were originally sold with products in them (like cigar boxes) or boxes that were simply made to look pretty. You might even specialize in boxes made for one purpose (like holding a deck of cards). A favorite kind of box collection includes only those boxes that have "secrets" — lots of other, smaller boxes, nested one inside another.

WHERE TO LOOK

Attics and basements, garage sales and swap meets, luggage and dime stores, gift and tobacco shops, the large, inexpensive import places like Pier One or Cost Plus, art and drugstores, and (if you can afford it) jewelry stores and boutiques — these are all treasure troves for the box collector.

Around Saint Valentine's Day, you'll find wonderful, heart-shaped boxes. At Easter there are egg-shaped ones, well worth collecting. Souvenir boxes can be picked up wherever you travel, and they sometimes tell a lot about the place. (In Florida they sell shell-covered boxes; in the Pacific Northwest, lovely ones covered with pine needles; in lake country, boxes made of birch bark.)

THINGS YOU'LL NEED

You may need boxes to hold your more perishable boxes! Big, see-through, plastic shoe boxes are good, and not too expensive.

GETTING IT TOGETHER

Showing off your box collection is easiest if you make risers for some of your shelves. These are small platforms or steps made out of wood or cardboard and covered with cloth. You can even use a cracker box (covered with pretty paper or cloth) to hold tiny, lightweight boxes. By placing a riser on the *back* part of a shelf, you can be sure that the boxes in back can be seen *over* the ones in front.

Cloth-covered or highly carved boxes are dust collectors, and since dust isn't good for *your* collection, keep these fragile items under wraps, in closed cupboards or see-through boxes!

GOOD, BETTER, BEST

You can look at boxes in at least three ways:

1. As pieces of sculpture, or "packaging art." Either the shape pleases you, or it doesn't! Tastes vary and what you *like* is what is good.

2. There are boxes that may have an ordinary shape, but wonderful color and design on the printed outside. These decorative boxes were generally made to sell what was in the box, and they are

valued as "advertising art." (Mind you, the advertising on the outside can be wonderful and colorful or it can be drab, boring, or ugly. Once again, either you like it or you don't—that's your choice.)

3. A box can be important for historical reasons. It can be dull and plain to look at, but interesting because of age or because of the product that it once contained.

THE COLLECTOR'S DREAM

In cigar *tins*, the rarest of all is the Buster Brown cigar can picturing Buster Brown with his dog and his dad. It was made in the mid-1920s, but for some reason there are only *two* known examples anywhere!

Boxes with humorous subjects on the outside, or with pictures of a particular period in history—for example, patriotic boxes made in the 1880s or '90s, with eagles and flags or other very American scenes and symbols—are valuable but still available for you to find at reasonable prices.

Best of all is a box that is lovely to touch, pretty to look at, *and* rare!

HELP! AND MORE HELP—

The Handbook of American Cigar Boxes by Tony Hyman; Arnot Art Museum, Elmira, New York.

The Tin Can Collector's Association is probably the largest club in the United States dealing with packaging. They put out a monthly newsletter, called *Tin-Type*, P.O. Box 4555, Denver, Colorado 80204.

Buttons/Badges

IT'S UP TO YOU

If you collect regular buttons (the kind you sew on clothes), you have lots to choose from. For example, you can specialize in buttons with pictures printed on them (like flags), buttons with different shapes (like animals or vegetables), or buttons all made out of a favorite material (bone, metal, ceramic, or papier-mâché).

If you are more interested in badges with a pin on the back, you can go after ones created for political campaigns or military awards, silly badges with funny sayings on them, badges given out by companies to advertise their products, or membership and club badges.

WHERE TO LOOK

Swap meets, garage sales and flea markets are good places, of course, but don't overlook the obvious. Old clothes in the attic might have lovely buttons sewn on—buttons made long ago, no longer available, and perhaps worth something.

If you collect political badges (the pin-on kind) you can write or visit a campaign headquarters and simply ask for one or two buttons. Be honest and tell them you're a collector and not necessarily a supporter. But you might promise to wear the button for a while before you pop it into your collection.

THINGS YOU'LL NEED

Small buttons or sets of buttons can be kept in small drawers or flat cases. Inexpensive jewel boxes or plastic toolchests are nice because you can see your goodies at a glance. Most button collectors like to have a special ruler marked in millimeters, lines, and lignes, for measuring the size of buttons.

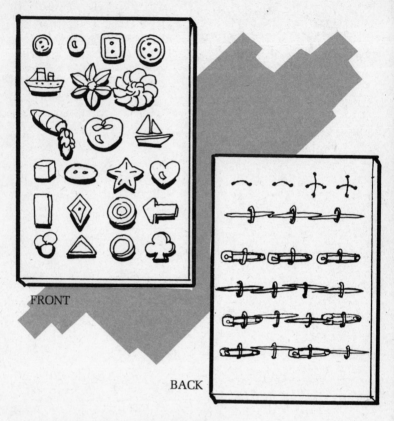

FRONT

BACK

GETTING IT TOGETHER

The easiest way to mount your buttons or pin-backs is to poke small holes in cardboard, stick the back part of the button through the hole, and attach it in back of the cardboard. (Either take a stitch through the button or the button shank (the loop in back of the button) or stick a safety pin or toothpick through it to hold the button in place.) You can use a large sheet of poster board or cut it into small squares to fit in a drawer.

GOOD, BETTER, BEST

Buttons become more valuable when a particular kind is

made for only a short time and then the run is discontinued. For example, my father who is a magician collected ceramic buttons with large wire shanks on the back, which were made in the shape of playing cards. They were manufactured in Europe for only one year. Because no more of them are being made and because lots of people scrounge around for things related to playing cards and magic, these buttons are now becoming valuable.

Pin-back badges made just for a campout or meeting, ones given out at a one-time-only sporting event or to honor a special team, and badges that have funny timely sayings or cartoons on them—these are all worth stowing away.

THE COLLECTOR'S DREAM

In political buttons, it's a Cox-Roosevelt pin-back of 1924, advertising the fact that Cox was running for president of the United States.

HELP! AND MORE HELP—

Hobbies Magazine, 1006 South Michigan Avenue, Chicago, Illinois 60605.

Political Collector Newspaper, 444 Lincoln Street, York, Pennsylvania 17404.

American Political Item Collectors, 1054 Sharpsburg Drive, Huntsville, Alabama 35803.

American Society of Military Insignia Collectors, 744 Warfold Avenue, Oakland, California 94610.

National Button Society, 2825 Hampshire Road, Cleveland Heights, Ohio 44118.

Clippings

IT'S UP TO YOU

It's fun to try to gather all the cartoon strips of a daily comic page series (like Peanuts). You might prefer to clip out newspaper and magazine articles about certain

subjects (dancing or magic, or whatever interests you), news stories about certain personalities (say, the president of the United States), or professions (TV stars, or athletes, or veterinarians).

Your collection of clippings could end up being a first-rate record of what is happening in ecology, or you could put together a sensational scrapbook showing all the sides of a political issue, or everything you can find about the country your family came from.

You might be on the lookout for information and pictures to support a hobby, such as pictures of new car designs to help you in your miniature model making, or magazine articles showing antique dolls to help you in making costumes.

THINGS YOU'LL NEED

Use loose-leaf scrapbooks so that you can move the pages around and add other stuff. Albums with a plastic cover sheet for each page (to hold the clippings down

without gluing) are best. A gadget called Clippit, found in most stationery stores, helps remove articles quickly from newspapers without using scissors. A dull pointed knife, pliers for removing staples from magazines, and plastic bags or envelopes for holding old clippings will be useful.

GETTING IT TOGETHER

Always clip out the corner of another page that has the date of the newspaper or magazine where you got the clipping. If this isn't possible, write the date and source on a separate piece of paper and keep it with your clipping. NEVER paste your clippings into a book. Put them under plastic. And whenever possible, frame 'em or put 'em up on a corkboard for all to see.

HELP! AND MORE HELP—

World Encyclopedia of Comics by Maurice Horn; Chelsea House Publishers, New York. This has all kinds of information for comic strip collectors, especially for people who have a particular hobby or interest.

Dolls/Puppets

IT'S UP TO YOU

Doll collections are as varied as the people who collect them. Some folks like to round up dolls from various countries. Others gather tiny dolls, or huge dolls, or dolls made at the turn of the century, or ones crafted out of one special material (such as wood, paper, cardboard, cloth or china). There are doll fanciers who are always on the lookout for dolls of famous people, or dolls that can do certain things, like swim, talk or walk.

Puppet collections that I have known and loved range from some that feature puppets from a certain country (for example, rod puppets from Indonesia or shadow puppets from China) to others specializing in marionettes (string puppets) only. And then there are the rest of my friends who collect puppets, puppets, puppets—finger puppets, hand puppets, rod and shadow puppets—you name it, they want it!

WHERE TO LOOK

Start with garage sales, secondhand stores, and (best of

all) your friends and neighbors. For more expensive dolls and puppets, poke around swap meets, toy stores, and shows sponsored by doll or puppet clubs.

Lots of cities have United Nations gift stores which sometimes carry dolls and puppets from foreign countries. Some towns have ethnic stores (say, Greek, Israeli, or Scotch) that sell all sorts of fascinating goods, including dolls and puppets, from that country.

HOW TO START

Any new doll should be kept complete with its wardrobe, extras, and the original box.

Build on your parents' collection. Let friends know that you want the dolls they've outgrown. Take those dolls and puppets that have been loved to death and fix 'em up. Tell everyone that you are a doll or puppet freak, and I'll bet that's what you'll receive as gifts. Wherever you go, buy for your collection rather than buying souvenirs. Tell traveling friends not to bother with postcards, but that small dolls would be appreciated.

GOOD, BETTER, BEST

Old dolls are more prized if they have a manufacturer's name on them, because that tells where they came from and the era in which they were made. (Most doll companies only existed for a limited number of years.)

Dolls of famous TV and movie stars are also generally made for one period of time only. Shirley Temple, Princess Elizabeth, and Sonja Henie dolls, made by Madame Alexander, were all popular in the 1930s and '40s. They're now worth lots! So are more recent character dolls, like the Cher and Captain Action dolls. The Shari Lewis doll, made by Madame Alexander in the mid-1960s, is now worth hundreds and hundreds of dollars, and I don't have a single copy! (Of course, I do have the original—me!)

All dolls are more valuable if they are in good condition, in the original box and complete with all available parts and accessories.

Many a collector's idea of heaven is to own all the versions of a classic doll, like Barbie.

First sold by Mattel in 1959, Barbie has had a different model each year since—1979 was a kissing Barbie, 1980 a Beauty Secrets Barbie, with hair down to her hips!

Some Barbie fanatics also try to round up all of Barbie's friends, including her boyfriend Ken, and her best friend Midge, as well as Barbie's little sister Skipper.

GETTING IT TOGETHER

Dolls can be put on stands and placed inside closed

cupboards or individual glass cases. Both dolls and puppets can be wrapped and laid to rest in cardboard boxes.

Marionettes should be put into separate plastic bags, with a "twisty" or rubber band on the outside of the bag around the strings, to keep them from tangling. Inside each bag, drop a packet of silica gel (camera stores have this) to prevent condensation and mildew.

I keep my antique rod and hand puppets upright and on display for all to see. Here's how: I stick the open part of the puppet over the neck of an empty bottle. The "skirt" of the puppet hides the bottle, and the neck of the bottle supports the puppet just beautifully.

HELP! AND MORE HELP—

Art of the Puppet by Bill Baird; Bonanza Books, Crown Publishers, New York.

Complete Book of Doll Collecting by Helen Young; G. P. Putnam's Sons, New York.

Flags/Emblems/ Patches

IT'S UP TO YOU

Countries all have flags. So do states, counties, and most cities and towns. There are company flags, pennants from teams in many sports, and banners representing scout troops, schools, and other organizations. You'll find all sorts of military pennants, signal flags and religious flags. Even amusement parks sell collectible pennants.

Emblems and patches range from military insignias, airline identification and scout merit and troop badges, to novelty badges showing monster faces and funny sayings.

THINGS YOU'LL NEED

Scrapbooks can be used for the flat embroidered emblems and patches. Double-faced tape will help keep them in place under the plastic coversheet.

You'll need long boxes for your flags, so they can be rolled rather than folded. If you hang flags, get little tags with strings on them and attach one to each flag. On it write where you got the flag, when, who won the game (if it's a team flag), and any other facts.

GETTING IT TOGETHER

Flags should be rolled on something round, like a mailing tube, and then slid into a cover, like a box, larger tube, or a cloth or plastic bag.

Badges and patches can be laid out in shallow drawers or trays, or attached with straight pins to a cloth-covered cardboard. One way to separate them is by type —say, all army items in one group, navy in another, and

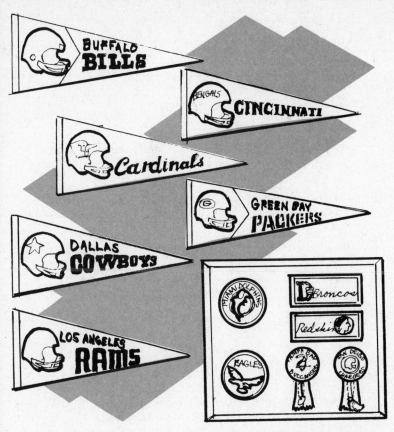

so on (if you have a military collection)—or you can display shoulder patches in one place, pocket emblems in another, and flags and pennants somewhere else.

GOOD, BETTER, BEST

Organizations that have been around for a long time (like the Boy Scouts, Girl Scouts or the army), change their badges, patches, emblems, and insignias every couple of years. Sometimes they just update the *design*. A new patch may be added and an old one dropped. Those old designs and emblems tend to increase in value. Not only do they become hard to find, but people who have been in the scouts or army may feel nostalgic about those organizations.

And the rule in all collecting is this: If there's not a lot of one item, and there are a lot of people who want it— it's in demand and worth more!

WHERE TO LOOK

Scrounge around in army-navy surplus stores, second-hand shops (especially those selling old uniforms), and souvenir stands wherever you go (even those in airports). And of course, rummage through garage sales, swap meets, and every attic you can get permission to search.

Ask friends in the Girl and Boy Scouts to keep you in mind as they attend special events and campouts. These often have special patches made for the occasion. Talk with older friends and relatives who used to be in the army. They may have just what you are looking for in a closet somewhere, and you just might be able to talk them out of it.

HELP! AND MORE HELP—

Flag Book of the United States by Whitney Smith; William Morrow & Co., New York, 1970, 1975.

Collector's News, Box 156, Grundy Center, Iowa 50638.

American Society of Military Insignia Collectors, 66 Golf Street, Newington, Connecticut 06111.

Games/Puzzles

IT'S UP TO YOU

A game collector might specialize in one kind of game only. That could be computer and video games, variations of Parchesi, playing cards, dice and dice cups, casino games, fantasy games, games that recreate famous battles, take-aparts, optical illusions, puzzles, jigsaw puzzles, even novel crossword puzzles (like the one that's 3-feet square).

Some game lovers try to dig up games associated with TV or movie characters they like (for example, Lone Ranger games). You may choose to collect just any old game. That's fine, too.

WHERE TO LOOK

Some people get tired of games and puzzles and are willing to give 'em away, if asked. Ask them! Other friends may feel they've outgrown this game or that one. Ask them! Garage sales are game goldmines. When kids grow up and move away from home, parents often get rid of old playthings, and you can scoop them up for very little.

Prices at swap meets may be higher, as dealers know what price a game or puzzle should bring. Make the rounds of stationery, toy, and department stores to pick up items missing from your collection and to keep up with new games and puzzles on the market.

Fantasy and war games are often sold *only* through hobby shops (rather than toy stores), and the people in hobby shops generally know all about playing and collecting in this very special area of hobby gaming.

GETTING IT TOGETHER

Start a card file with one card for each game or one for

each game *company*. List anything and everything the company makes. Check off the ones you own, so you'll know which of their products you *don't* have.

Try not to stack your games more than six to eight high or you'll put too much weight on the bottom one and crush the box. If space is tight and you have to stack smaller games on top of a large one, put a sheet of heavy cardboard over the large box to spread the weight.

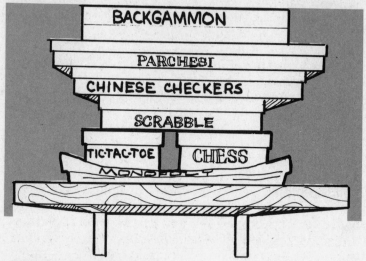

GOOD TO KNOW

People who know about hobby gaming (like Peter Olotka, creator of the new board game, Cosmic Encounter, in which players become alien characters and the point of the game is to move your various alien characters around the universe) say hobby gaming is mostly for older kids, say 12 and up. The field of hobby gaming includes:

    1. War games (like Starship Trooper and World War II).

    2. Fantasy games (for example, Travelers or Dungeons and Dragons).

    3. Board games (such as Cosmic Traveler, Diplomacy or Kingmaker).

4. Miniature gaming (various sets of rules all about how to set up tiny armies of toy soldiers and fight different battles).

HELP! AND MORE HELP—

A Player's Guide to Table Games by John Jackson; Stackpole Books, Harrisburg, Pennsylvania.

The Way to Play, Paddington Press Ltd., New York.

Gambler's Book Club, Box 4115, Las Vegas, Nevada 89106, has an extensive catalog of books on all sorts of games.

Games Magazine, P.O. Box 10145, Des Moines, Iowa 50340.

Fantasy and science fiction gaming magazines include *Area* (Simultations Publications), *Different Worlds* (Chaosium), *Dragon* (TSR Hobbies), *Dungeoneer* (Judges Guild), *Journal of Travellers' Aid Society* (Game Designers' Workshop), *Judges' Journal* (Judges Guild), *Sorceror's Apprentice* (Flying Buffalo), *Space Gamer* (Metagaming).

Among the wargaming magazines there are: *Campaign* (Avalon Enterprises), *Fire and Movement* (Baron Publishing), *General* (Avalon Hill Games), *Grenadier* (Game Designers' Workshop), *Moves* (Simultations Publications), *Strategy and Tactics* (Simultations Publications), *Wargamer's Digest* (McCoy Publications), *Wargaming* (Fantasy Games Unlimited).

TSR Hobbies, Inc., P.O. Box 756, Lake Geneva, Wisconsin 53147, has a catalog of fantasy games and additional materials.

Playing Card Collectors Association, 1511 West 6th Street, Racine, Wisconsin 53404.

Jewelry

IT'S UP TO YOU

People collect jewelry for many reasons. Some like to wear it. You always see these friends decked out in their collections of silver and turquoise American Indian jewelry, or covered with their tiny dangling charm bracelets and necklaces, or sporting funky pins from the 1940s.

Others like to have lots of *fine* jewelry because gold, silver, and real gemstones seem to be worth more and more as the years go by.

I know someone who spends his weekends tracking down jewelry that's not used much anymore (key-wind pocket watches, watchfobs, and old hatpins).

Some kids collect jewelry related to favorite TV and movie characters (Snoopy pins, Mickey Mouse watches, etc.).

If your family comes from another country you might specialize in arts and crafts from there. Perhaps you can put together a jewelry "starter set" by asking grandparents, older cousins and aunts. (Delicate Israeli filigree, Mexican silverwork, and Italian shell cameos are well worth having.)

A jewelry collection can be put together consisting of nothing but glass jewelry, or just rings, or just whatever else interests you.

WHERE TO LOOK

Check with family and friends for jewelry they don't want anymore.

Parents often have charms collected through the years, showing highpoints in their lives (a tiny baby charm given on the birth of a child, a little piano keyboard celebrating the winning of a music contest, a religious symbol such as a cross or Jewish star—given at the completion of religious studies). Some gals have wonderful memory bracelets with one dangling charm for each place they've visited on vacation and business.

GETTING IT TOGETHER

Inexpensive fabric cases, or wooden or plastic jewel boxes are available in most places. Toolchests (particularly plastic ones) are good storage units because they have so many small sections for separating this from that!

If you don't have any of those, wrap each piece of jewelry in tissue and put it into a small box. A number of small boxes, each with an identifying sticker, can then be put into a larger box. If you tuck your things away in a jewelry box, hang a tiny tag on each describing any facts you know about it. Set up a card file, with each card listing one item and telling where you got it, what you paid, where it was made, by whom, who owned it before you, etc.

Most charm collectors enjoy wearing parts of their collections. There are charmholders that display lots of charms on a chain around your neck all at the same time.

If your collection is precious (made of genuine gold and real gemstones, or really old), don't leave it around. It may not be there the next time you look!

Show off your rings on a handy ring holder made from an old glove, stuffed and pulled over the mouth of an old bottle, so it can stand upright on your dresser with rings on each finger.

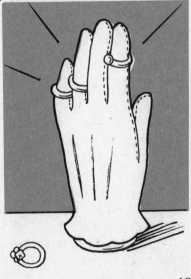

If you are the proud owner of lots of shiny costume jewelry, decorate your house at Christmas with all that sparkling stuff. Make a treasure tree. Out of green felt or paper, cut the outline of a pine tree. Attach it to a bulletin board, cork board, or piece of thick cardboard. Stick in lots of tiny hooks and dangle your goodies, the gaudier the better, as though they were Christmas ornaments.

HELP! AND MORE HELP—

Rings for the Finger by George Kunz; Dover Publications, New York.

Collector's News, Box 156, Grundy Center, Iowa 50638.

Grieger's Inc., 900 South Arroyo Parkway, Pasadena, California 91109. This dealer in jewelry findings and gems has a catalog that's free for the asking.

Gems and Minerals Magazine, P.O. Box 687, Mentone, California 94359, carries a lot of information and ads about jewelry.

Keys/Locks

IT'S UP TO YOU

You can specialize in just one type of key: *bit* keys, usually large and heavy, used to open old-fashioned door locks; *cylinder* keys—today's type of door key; or *stamped* keys—flat ones with notches cut into them, often used for cashboxes or suitcases.

You can keep your eyes open for unusual keys like the fancy ones used for winding antique watches and clocks, or magnetic keys.

There's also the fascinating possibility of collecting locks and locking devices—such as handcuffs and leg-irons, padlocks, miniature locks, and locks with unusual keys—or even secret methods of opening *without* keys.

WHERE TO LOOK

Somewhere in your home, there may be a drawer or box or plastic bag full of discarded keys. Since it's very easy to lose a key, many people keep old keys, just in case! (I know I do.) Ask friends and relatives if they will give you their unwanted keys—the ones that don't really match up with any lock in the house.

Poke around garage sales. Ask in keyshops. (In my neighborhood the key maker gives spares and extra keys to kids who come in.)

Locks are an especially interesting hobby for young people who are good with their hands. Ask friends who travel to foreign countries to pick up samples of locks used abroad. When you go to towns other than your own, look in the phone book, and then check out locksmiths. Hunt for key and lock samples that you don't already have in your collection.

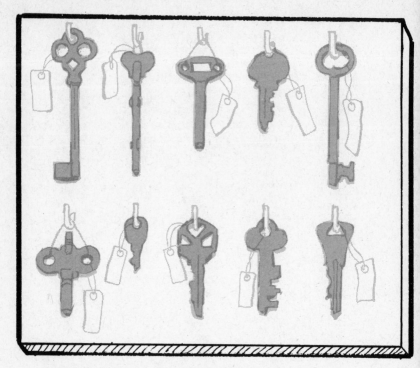

GETTING IT TOGETHER

Tag each key. List the lock it goes with, the manufacturer, type of metal, where you got it, and approximately when it was made or first used. Each key can be hung on a hook fastened to a sheet of pegboard. Or you can put keys on a ring with other keys, and then hang up the ring.

The most interesting of your locks can be displayed on shelves. The rest of your locks can be stored away in boxes.

TALKING THE LANGUAGE

- Bit—the part of a key that turns the tumblers in the lock.
- Blank—an uncut key; unfinished, before it is cut to fit a lock.

- Bow—the handle of a key.
- Case ward—a piece of metal on the inside of a lock that fits through a cut in the key so the key can then turn in the lock.
- Code—a group of letters and/or numbers to tell a locksmith how to cut a key to match a certain lock.
- Keyway—the design and shape of a keyhole.
- Master key—one key that will open a number of different locks, each one of which also has its own key.
- Operating key—a key that fits only one particular lock.
- Plug—the round core of a lock cylinder which turns when the key is turned.

HELP! AND MORE HELP—

Story of Locks by Walter Buehr; Charles Scribner's Sons, New York.

History of Locks, Yale & Towne, Inc., Chrysler Building, New York 10017. This is a free booklet on the history and working of locks.

American Lock Collectors Association, 14010 Cardwell, Livonia, Michigan 48154.

Lock Museum of America, Terryville, Connecticut.

There is a series of books called the *Thomas Register of Manufacturers* in the reference section of many libraries. Under the heading "Locks," it lists companies that make keys and locks. You can write to the company that interests you for information about when a key you have was made, what lock it was made for, the material used, and so on.

Kits

IT'S UP TO YOU

The Hobby Industry of America took a five-year poll and discovered that *model-building* is the biggest of all hobbies in the country—with plane, car and ship models the most popular.

Other models you can build and collect include western kits (wagons, stagecoaches, western towns), models of movie characters (like the robots from *Star Wars*), television stars (such as the put-it-together-yourself Six Million Dollar Man), other famous people, monsters, old-time types of transportation. The list of kits or plans that you can buy is huge!

Kits are usually made from plastic, wood or both, and they come in a variety of scales.

Scale means the size of the finished model in relation to the real, life-sized car, person, or what-have-you. For example, if the scale of something is 1/12, that means that one inch equals 12 inches or one foot. (This scale is often used for doll houses and doll house furniture.)

You can choose to make all your models of one size (for cars and planes, the most popular scales are 1/24 and 1/32), or you may prefer to put together all models of one kind (monsters, or sailing ships, or whatever makes you happy).

WHERE TO LOOK

Hobby and craft shops and toystores sell many different kinds of kits. Magazine stands often display a number of issues covering different types of models, and you can send mail orders to the dealers advertising in them.

HOW TO START

Pick a simple kit, preferably of plastic, and put it

together. As you're making this one, you'll get ideas about your next. Perhaps next time you'll explore a whole different idea or subject. Experiment with scale— find a scale that you like best. Smaller scales are harder to work on, and so are kits that have lots and lots of details.

Try to finish your first kit before starting on a second, and don't be in a hurry. If you take the time, you'll enjoy making it as much as you enjoy *having* the finished product. And it does take time to make a model look its best.

HELP! AND MORE HELP—

Junior American Modeler Magazine, 733 15th Street, N.W., Washington, D.C. 20005.

International Plastic Modelers Society, Box 2555, Long Beach, California 90801.

Magic

IT'S UP TO YOU

Because my father is a magician, I have many friends whose apartments and houses are crammed with magic collections. Each is different! Here are some of the many ways a magic collection can be brought together. You can specialize in:

- Equipment—*pocket tricks*, different versions of *the classics of magic* (like the Linking Rings), *basic club magic apparatus* (usually boxes and tubes), or just the secret little *gimmicks* of this tricky trade (like thumb tips).
- Printed information — instructions, manuscripts describing the effects of tricks or the routines and patter done with them, clippings about magic and magicians, and blueprints showing how to build magical apparatus.
- Publicity—photographs, programs, and posters advertising magicians and/or their shows.
- Magic sets—groups of tricks offered together in a box or package, and made by a magic company or as advertising by a manufacturer.
- Things related to magic — rabbits (statues, dolls, pictures, etc.), playing cards, high hats.

WHERE TO LOOK

The obvious places are magic and novelty shops, some hobby and craft shops, swap meets and garage sales, new and used bookstores, and the library. Also look on the backs of cereal packages and other grocery items for special magic kits offered by the manufacturers.

Young magicians often trade tricks with one another, so try to join a magic club. The greatest fun in magic is sharing your hobby with others.

GETTING IT TOGETHER

If you get a new trick, keep the instructions either *with* the trick itself or in an alphabetical file. Keep small items in their original envelopes or boxes, and put them in larger boxes marked alphabetically or by category (card tricks, rope effects, etc.).

TALKING THE LANGUAGE

- Breakaway—a piece of apparatus designed to fall apart in a spectator's hand.
- Divination — a trick that involves discovering which object has been secretly selected.
- Dropper—a secret device for holding some object out of sight.
- Fake—a piece of apparatus made to look like an everyday object.
- Houlette—an open box for holding a deck of cards.
- Levitation — making an object or person seem to float in the air.
- Production—the appearance of an object or person.
- Pull—a secret pulley for whisking an object out of sight.
- Silk — magician's word for scarf or handkerchief, because it always *used* to be made of silk.
- Transformation—changing an object or person into a different object or person.
- Vanish—when something or someone disappears.

HELP! AND MORE HELP—

Genii Magazine, P.O. Box 36038, Los Angeles, California 90019.

International Brotherhood of Magicians, 28 North Main Street, Kenton, Ohio 43326.

Menus/Placemats

IT'S UP TO YOU

You can try to round up one menu from every restaurant in your town, or one from every city in the country. You might try to gather only children's menus or ones from health food restaurants. Perhaps menus from all kinds of foreign food restaurants will interest you—or just sample listings from Japanese, or Mexican, or Greek eating places.

Some people collect menus from restaurants on board trains or steamships. Others want to have one menu from every fast food restaurant they visit, say, in the course of a long trip.

Old menus, oversized menus (bound like books), those made of unusual materials, or handwritten, or for special local events (such as church dinners or weddings) — these are all nifty ideas for starting a menu collection.

WHERE TO LOOK

Although menus cost restaurants money to make, the owners and managers are often delighted to give you a sample menu for your collection. It's good publicity! It keeps the restaurant's name before your eyes, and when others riffle through your collection, it brings the restaurant's name to their attention, too.

Get into the habit of asking the waiter, waitress, or manager for a menu whenever you eat out.

Write to famous restaurants in distant places. Ask for a menu. Tell 'em why you want it, and include a big (8 × 10) stamped, self-addressed envelope.

Ask your friends and your parents' friends to help you gather copies from all over. People love to add to other folks' collections.

Paper placemats are easy to get. Just ask and you'll be given a clean one to take home.

GETTING IT TOGETHER

Paper placemats are full of identifying clues. They often

tell not only the name of the restaurant but what is served by the chain. Add a little sticker to the back of each, noting when you were there, what you ate, and with whom.

These paper placemats and many menus make dandy wall decorations.

If you decide to put your collection into notebooks, *don't paste them in!* Wherever possible, use photomount corners and hinges, so that people can read what's on the back of the menu as well as the front. See the chapter on stamps for an example of how hinges work (page 90).

Whether you store your menus and placemats in notebooks or file boxes, they can be grouped geographically (where they come from), alphabetically (by the name of the restaurant), by the kind of food, or any other way that makes sense to you.

THINGS TO LOOK FOR

Some nice features that make a menu a pleasure to have, look at and touch include:

1. A printing process where the ink rises above the paper because it's so thick. That's called *thermography*.

2. Letters or designs pushed higher than the rest of the paper with no ink or color on them. That's *blind embossing*.

3. Shiny printing (usually in gold or silver) stamped on the cover of the menu. The technique is *heatstamping*.

HELP! AND MORE HELP—

Mobil Travel Guides, Simon & Schuster, New York. Available in most libraries.

Collector's News, Box 156, Grundy Center, Iowa 50638 carries a section called Paper Items.

IT'S UP TO YOU

Collecting miniatures is very satisfying because you can create a tiny world, complete in almost every way, and you are in charge. Miniature dolls, doll houses, and doll house furniture have been popular for hundreds of years.

Lots of grownups have huge armies of tiny toy soldiers; others are wild about military equipment. (Some play war games with their little warriors. See miniature gaming, page 47.)

There are very serious collectors of railroad scenes, tiny musical instruments and miniature cars. These cars have become extremely popular—not only the detailed models for admiring (like Matchbox and Dinky Toys) but also the slot-cars and radio-controlled cars.

You might choose to collect all tiny objects of one size or scale, so that all look as though they belong together. On the other hand, you might decide to collect toy soldiers, tiny animals, or little trains, regardless of their size.

WHERE TO LOOK

Many craft and hobby shops can tell you about local clubs, shows and displays. Keep looking in dime and department stores, souvenir counters, and gift departments of drugstores. Garage sales and swap meets will have a lot to offer in the way of miniatures. Check the classified telephone directories for shops that specialize in miniatures. They will be under the heading of Hobby and Model Supplies.

And do tell everybody that you're collecting miniatures. When your friends and relations know what you like, they really enjoy picking out gifts for you.

GETTING IT TOGETHER

You'll need lots and lots of shelves on which to display your miniatures, and risers which you place on shelves to add more useable surfaces are very helpful.

Some miniatures (such as tiny sailing ships and things covered in fabric) are hard to clean if they get dusty. Try to keep these inside a closed cabinet or behind glass.

If you collect dollhouse furniture, make yourself a single room and decorate it with furniture all in one scale. (Just cut down the sides of a cardboard carton, and *after* your room is fully furnished, attach a roof.)

GOOD, BETTER, BEST

A miniature collection is most admired when everything is in perfect condition and in perfect scale to other items placed near it or in your collection.

THE COLLECTOR'S DREAM

The absolute tops would be to find a complete miniature house or scene dating from the 1800s or 1700s. They're still around but very scarce.

Another knockout would be to get a scene made by one of the great craftsmen who created in miniature for famous collectors like Duke Albrecht V of Bavaria or Mrs. James Ward Thorne of Chicago.

HELP! AND MORE HELP—

Nutshell News Magazine, 10 Clifton House, Clifton, Virginia 22024.

Model Soldier Manual by Peter J. Blum; Imrie/Risley Miniatures, Ballston Spa, New York 12020.

National Association of Miniature Enthusiasts, P.O. Box 2621, Anaheim, Califiornia 92804.

Money

IT'S UP TO YOU

There are lots of ways to become a numismatist. (Yes, that's what you'll turn into if you start collecting money as a hobby.)

Young people sometimes begin by specializing in one or two American coins (say, pennies and nickels). Next, they branch out to other United States coins or paper money, foreign money, or ancient coins.

If you want a real challenge, look for errors—coins or bills with mistakes on them (incorrectly stamped, struck twice, blank on one side, or with a goof in the design).

You can even specialize in souvenir money—miniature coins and frankly-fake bills printed for advertising and novelty purposes (like wooden nickels and the huge dollar bills that magicians give away).

HOW TO START

At some dime stores and most coin stores, you can get single-page holders or albums to display coins.

Check the change in your pocket every day. Make

Are you a numismatist?

LIBERTY

arrangements with your parents and friends to check their change, too. Look at the design, date, mint mark and silver content. In the past, many countries have used pure silver in their coins. U.S. dimes, quarters and half dollars were silver until 1964. Then they became "sandwich" coins, containing layers of various metals. The dime and quarter sandwiches had no silver at all. The half dollar sandwiches had some silver from 1965 to 1969. Now there is no silver in any U.S. coins. That's why the date of the coin can tell you a lot more than just when it was made.

THINGS YOU'LL NEED

Start with a magnifying glass and some coin envelopes, and add coin folders or display books, guidebooks and dealer's catalogs.

GOOD TO KNOW

Don't clean any coins. Put them all, even if they're new and uncirculated when you buy them, into coin holders and try not to handle them with your fingers.

THINGS TO LOOK FOR

Civil War coins (called copperheads) are lucky finds. So are U.S. bills of $1, $5, and $20 with the word HAWAII printed on the back. (These "Hawaiian" notes were used there during World War II.) Look for a second design struck onto a coin already stamped with one design (this is called an overstrike). Also look for a coin or bill with a mistake on the side with the main design (this is called a mule).

TALKING THE LANGUAGE

- Field—the flat surface of a coin between the design of the head and the writing along the edge.

- Legend—the words written around the coin inside the border.
- Lettered edge—lettering milled into the edge of a coin rather than reeding.
- Milled edge—a thick, raised edge; not to be confused with a "reeded edge."
- Mint mark—a small letter or symbol indicating the mint (or coin factory) where the coin was struck.
- Mint set—one coin of each denomination issued by a given mint for a given year.
- Patina—the darkening of copper coins as they age.
- Proof set—set of coins, one of each denomination, struck by special dies and for sale to collectors only; they're never circulated.
- Reeded edge—notches running across the edge of a coin.

GOOD, BETTER, BEST

- Uncirculated—in perfect condition, showing no signs of wear, as issued from the mint.

- Very fine—slightly used, almost mint condition.
- Fine—date clear but edges slightly worn.
- Very good—legible but definitely worn.
- Good—worn, but design and lettering still plain.
- Fair—considerably worn.

HOT TIP

For a good investment, keep your eyes open for certain African and South American coins. Some of these countries mint so few that the coins will probably increase in value. Look in the coin guidebooks or ask in your local coin store for the specific countries worth collecting.

HELP! AND MORE HELP—

Guidebook of U.S. Coins by R. S. Yeoman; Whitman Publishing Co., Racine, Wisconsin.

Coin World Weekly, 911 Vandermark Road, Sidney, Ohio 45363.

U.S. Coin Exchange, 1327 Santa Monica Boulevard, Santa Monica, California 90404.

American Numismatic Association, P.O. Box 2366, Colorado Springs, Colorado 80901.

Historical Paper Money Research Institute, Box 187, Bridgeport, Pennsylvania 19404, has a long list of inexpensive booklets on paper money.

Photographs

IT'S UP TO YOU

You can collect snapshots of people you know and places you've been, pictures of famous people, movie stills, old photographs (say, from before the 1900s), or a particular kind of photo (like transparencies, black-and-white prints, sepia tones, daguerrotypes, tintypes, or glass negatives). You might snoop around for pictures relating to your hobby (magic? rollerskating?) or for war pictures. Photography's been around since the Civil War, and there are lots of pictures of soldiers, in and out of action.

WHERE TO LOOK

Many famous people will send a signed photograph if you write for it, especially if you include return postage. Second-hand bookstores often have a box or two of photos. Check with the theater managers in your town. Perhaps they'll save the movie advertising photos for you if you'll come by every week to pick them up. Ask the local camera shop owner for any prints packed away that you could have; these could be advertising photos, or prints that customers never picked up.

For particular subjects (cars, dolls, etc.) write to the public relations departments of various manufacturers.

The comic book shows and fairs usually have some dealers with movie and movie star photos for sale.

THINGS YOU'LL NEED

You'd better get some photomount corners and albums or albums with plastic-covered pages. Never paste the photos in place! Next to each photo, tape a caption (a description of who's in the photo, where it was taken, by whom, when, etc.). Whenever possible, frame your photos and let them brighten up a wall.

GETTING IT TOGETHER

Here's a clever way to display family photos and bring back the times when they were taken: Clip out a newspaper headline of an important current event. Fasten it to the same page, along with photos of that week.

If you are collecting your own photographs, and you have too many to keep 'em in albums, start a file. (Shoeboxes or larger boxes are perfect.) File your pictures as you take them, and label the boxes by month and year. Filing your prints will guarantee that you can put your hands on the one you want in a minute!

Make an index. List every photograph you have in each box (say, "Thanksgiving, 1980, John making a pig of himself" or whatever else will describe the contents of the picture).

Throw or give away any pictures that aren't good. Just keep the best.

Color prints and slides will fade if they are exposed to any kind of light or dampness. Store them in cool, dark, dry places. The color in your pictures is said to be able to last thirty years or more if protected.

Incidentally, well-made black-and-white prints are supposed to last 100 years. I only hope you're around to check up on whether this is true about your prints.

GOOD TO KNOW

NEVER write on the back of a photograph or on another sheet of paper when a photo is underneath. You'll leave an indented impression on the photo and ruin its looks forever. Don't glue a photo in place because many glues will leak through the paper and spot the picture.

TALKING THE LANGUAGE

- Bleed—when there are no white margins on a print and the picture goes all the way to the edge of the paper.
- Collodion plate—a negative developed on a square of glass covered with collodion.
- Daguerrotype—first practical photographic prints used until about the 1860s.
- Glossy—a print with a hard, shiny look.
- Matte—a print finish that is dull, not shiny.
- RC paper—a print paper coated with resin to give a hard finish.
- Sepia—a print in tones of brown instead of gray.

HELP! AND MORE HELP—

Photo Collector's Guide by Lee Witkin; Addison House, New York.

Photographic Historical Society of New York, P. O. Box 1839, Radio City Station, New York, New York 10019.

Postcards/ Stationery

IT'S UP TO YOU

Last summer we asked 675 campers (in three different camps) what they were collecting. The biggest item among the girls was *stationery*. They were trading single sheets, each trying to get as many different kinds of stationery as they could. What the girls wanted most were sheets with pictures of characters (like Snoopy), pretty flowers, and designs.

Lots of people around the world collect stationery. Even more specialize in *postcards*.

Some look for picture postcards—from various far-away places, or relating to special events like world fairs or winter festivals, or with comic pictures and sayings, or dealing with animals or a favorite hobby (like musical instruments or hot-air balloons). I even have a friend who collects the advertising postcards showing pictures of ventriloquists with their dummies!

Postcard collections featuring TV and movie characters (like Mickey Mouse or Kermit the Frog) are very popular. Flower-lovers hunt for picture postcards put out in Mississippi when the azaleas are in bloom, or in Washington, D.C. during cherry blossom time.

Collecting older postcards is really very interesting because the scenes or the pictures show how different the world used to be, while the written messages on the other side show how little people really have changed.

Postcard collecting can include the ones specially printed by the postal service.

You might even look for the preprinted envelopes and aerograms from the postal service. (An aerogram is a single piece of paper that is to be written on and then folded, sealed and addressed to be mailed.)

WHERE TO LOOK

Check with friends and family. Most everybody has old cards and letters tucked away somewhere. Second-hand and Salvation Army stores often have a box or two of old cards. (Look for old-fashioned greeting cards and party invitations too.) Garage sales are a super source. If you don't see any cards on display, ask about them.

Souvenir stands and stationery stores carry a wide variety of subjects in their cards, and you'll almost always find one or two to match your collection.

Write to hotels and motels. They all have special cards. You can also write to the chamber of commerce of any community and ask them to send you a souvenir postcard. In all cases, include return postage.

HOW TO START

Go through Christmas cards received by your family and keep the ones you like, or the cards dealing with your particular subject. Let family, friends and teachers know that you would be happy if they sent you postcards when they travel.

GETTING IT TOGETHER

Hobby shops sometimes carry special postcard albums with slits in each page for holding the corners of the cards. Of course, you can use photomount corners instead, in regular albums. Another way to organize your postcards and stationery is in shoeboxes. Cut cardboard dividers that stick up above everything else, to separate and group your goodies.

GOOD, BETTER, BEST

Obviously, old cards have more value than new ones. It's especially nice if they were written on, long ago, and mailed so they are clearly dated. If you lay your hands on some old cards, don't remove the stamps. Sometimes

they increase the value, and the cancellation mark on the stamp itself may help you figure out the date of the card.

To display cards on a bulletin board, slip the edges of the card under thumbtacks. Don't put a tack through the card, as the hole will make it worth a lot less.

HELP! AND MORE HELP—

Postcard Guide to Tuck Postcards by Sally Carver, 179 South Street, Chestnut Hill, Massachusetts 02167. Tuck is the name of one of the largest manufacturers of picture postcards.

United States Postalcard Catalog by George Martin; VanDahl Publishers, Box 10, Albany, Oregon 77321.

American Postcard Journal, Box 562, Westhaven, Connecticut 06516.

Collector's News, Box 156, Grundy Center, Iowa 50638.

Collecting Postcards in Colour by W. Duval; Blandford Press, Dorset, England.

Recordings

IT'S UP TO YOU

Some people collect old records. Any old records. Others hunt for recordings of one kind of music (big bands, early opera, or early rock like the Beatles). If you are building on your parents' old records, you might be able to specialize in just one singer (like Elvis Presley) or on hits of the 1940s, or on records that were in the Top Ten over the past many years.

Some record collectors concentrate on cassettes or cartridges, or look for wire recordings (these were used immediately after World War II).

If you want to tackle a really tough hobby, you can search for the original phonograph cylinders made shortly after Edison invented the phonograph.

WHERE TO LOOK

Almost everybody's record cabinet, attic, or garage will have something to offer you. Check around your home and in the neighborhood. Next, see what you can stumble upon at garage sales, Salvation Army and Goodwill stores. Then move on to secondhand stores and swap meets (they know value and are likely to be more expensive).

Some cities have record dealers that specialize in old records. Check the classified telephone directories.

THINGS YOU'LL NEED

Invest in a good silicone cleaning cloth and a brush (you can get both from a record store).

You'll need sturdy shelves, at least 12 inches deep, or boxes turned on their sides, in which to store the records. Don't use wire racks to hold your first-rate records, as they are more liable to warp.

Get small stickers and label each section of the shelf, so you'll know what's where!

GETTING IT TOGETHER

Flat records should be in individual slip jackets, or better yet in record albums. Record stores sell "stock sleeves," which are jackets for single records and are made of heavier paper than the jacket that comes with the record.

Store records on edge, not flat, and in a cool place away from heaters and sunlight.

Always handle records by their edges, as oil from your fingers can rot the grooves. Set up a card file with one card for each single or album.

GOOD, BETTER, BEST

To keep your albums in their best condition always put them back in their jacket or album as soon as you've finished playing them. Here's how some collectors grade the condition of their records:

- New minus — almost new, looks good and plays well.
- E plus — slightly worn, and if there is a scratch, it doesn't affect the sound.
- E — bad, very worn, scratchy.

HELP! AND MORE HELP—

55 Years of Recorded Country/Western Music by Jerry Osborn; O'Sullivan Woodside & Co., Phoenix, Arizona.

Record Album Price Guide by Jerry Osborn; O'Sullivan Woodside & Co., Phoenix, Arizona.

Record Collector's Price Guide by Jerry Osborn; O'Sullivan Woodside & Co., Phoenix, Arizona.

Hobbies Magazine, 1006 South Michigan Avenue, Chicago, Illinois 60605.

Rocks

IT'S UP TO YOU

Some folks try to turn up samples of all the rocks found in their area or state. Your collection might consist of rocks that will fit into one-inch, clear plastic boxes. You might specialize in just fossils (rocks with imprints of prehistoric animals or plants in them). Depending on where you live, you might choose to collect geodes (lumpy ball-shaped stones with crystals inside).

A friend of mine who travels for business takes plastic bags and glass jars with her everywhere, because she is making an enormous collection of all of the different *sands* found around the world.

Whatever it is you choose to collect, you will probably have a lot to try for. Even if you just gather crystals, there are over 300 different kinds!

WHERE TO LOOK

You can start in your own backyard, or on the nearest plot of bare ground. Find out what other rock hounds are discovering in your area. Then read up on *that* so you'll know it when you see it. Ask *where* the collectors are going to find rocks in your community. When you get there, you'll see where others have dug, and that's a good place for you to start.

Carry a hammer with you, and knock the corners off the rocks you find to see if they are, indeed, what you think they are. (Many rocks are hard to identify in the beginning because the outside skin is so dirty.)

When you find a rock or geode that you think might be a good one, you can always take it to a rock shop and have them cut it for you with a diamond saw.

Keep your eyes open as you travel. Good rocks can be found on beaches, hillsides, and open banks where the road cuts through a hill. Don't forget lakesides, river-beds, gravel pits or rock quarries, building sites, the desert, or any other kind of open country.

The most important thing to remember about rock hounding is this: Always go with someone else. NEVER go alone into quarries, the desert, or the mountains.

If you have a choice, get your sample as big as your hand so the details are all easy to see.

HOW TO START

When you've found a sample you want, clean off a spot on back, attach a sticker or tab to it, and number it. Put that same number in your notebook, along with scratch notes about where you found it and what other rocks you saw nearby.

Many minerals are only found in certain parts of the world, and often one or two spots have the best quality of that stone. For example, you may live in the perfect spot to find, say, jade or fossils. Talk to other rock fan-ciers and discover what good stuff exists just a stone's throw away from your home.

GETTING IT TOGETHER

After cleaning your specimens and figuring out what they are (use a rock guidebook), make out a file card with the date of the find, the exact location, whether it was loose or had to be freed, the complete identification, any peculiarities, and where it can be found in your collec-tion.

Show off your bigger rocks on shelves. Risers will come in handy, but they'll have to be made sturdily, of wood.

As you get more and more involved in rock hunting, you may want to try to get a tumbler so you can polish your own rocks. But until then, rock shops will polish your finds for you. (A number of small stones of the same type of hardness are put into the tumbler barrel,

along with water and powdered abrasives. The tumbler is turned by a motor for days or even weeks. The rocks are then inspected and if necessary tumbled again with finer abrasives, in order to get a smooth polish.)

GOOD, BETTER, BEST

A mineral that is pure is considered excellent. So is one that has an unusual "something" about it. A pure calcite crystal is worth more to a collector than one with a little line of feldspar in it. On the other hand, a piece of amber with a fossil insect on the inside is much more interesting than a plain piece of amber.

HELP! AND MORE HELP—

The Young Rockhound's Handbook by W.R.C. Shedenhelm; G. P. Putnam's Sons, New York.

Gems and Minerals Magazine, 1767 Capri Avenue, Mentone, California 92359.

Grieger's Inc., 900 South Arroyo Parkway, Pasadena, California 91109, has a free guide to collecting and working with rocks.

Shells

WHERE TO LOOK

Shells are getting harder and harder to come by. Because the world is so overpopulated, even beaches in really remote places are being stripped of good specimens. In some areas, it's against the law to take *anything*—shells, driftwood, even stones—off the beach.

Where it's O.K. to gather shells, your best bet is to check beaches for days after a storm. Then, the actions of tides and currents will have stranded some shell dwellers high and dry on the beaches, and the little critters will have deserted their shells in order to get back into the water.

DO NOT collect shells that have live creatures in them. All shore states have laws against taking live specimens, and these are enforced by very large fines or imprisonment! (The only exceptions are food mollusks, like clams, and you must have a fishing license in order to take them home.)

HOW TO START

The easiest way is to buy a beginner's assortment from a dealer, who will sell you lots and lots of shells for much less money than if you were to buy them separately. You can do this at a shell shop or by mail order from companies that advertise in shell magazines.

Most kids start with *cowrie* shells. They are inexpensive, and there are so many different kinds of cowries! They also have thicker and harder shells than most others. That's why it's possible to find more of them that are all in one piece.

Get a good shell book. Enjoy the gorgeous pictures and learn all the scoop about the different kinds of shells —what they're called and where they come from.

THINGS YOU'LL NEED

Plastic pails can be used to hold hard-shelled specimens. Get egg cartons or separate boxes for delicate ones. You'll need a short-length, stiff wire for cleaning sand and glop out of the shell, and both a soft brush and a hard one for making it look as beautiful as possible. A small shell book or field manual will come in handy (to carry on the beach with you, so you'll know what you're looking at). Also carry a tiny notebook and pencil. Keep these together in a see-through plastic bag so they're ready to go when you are.

GETTING IT TOGETHER

When you pick up shells, make a note for each, telling where you got it, how far from the water, whether it was low or high tide, the type of ground (sand, rocks, or in a tidepool), and the date (so you'll know the time of year).

Your finds can be kept in the separate compartments of egg cartons, in individual boxes, or in the lids of large boxes, lined with cotton or cloth.

Large hard-shelled items look lovely displayed like fruit in woven straw baskets. (These make terrific table centerpieces.)

HELP! AND MORE HELP—

Seashells of North America, A Golden Field Guide; Western Publishing Company, Golden Press, New York.

Shell Collector's Handbook by A. Hyatt Verrill; G. P. Putnam's Sons, New York.

Check your local bookstore because each area of the United States has a field guide to its own shells.

Hawaii Shell News Magazine, P.O. Box 10391, Honolulu, Hawaii 96816.

Hobbies Magazine, 1006 South Michigan Avenue, Chicago, Illinois 60605.

Of Sea and Shore Magazine, P.O. Box 33, Port Gamble, Washington 98364.

Pacific Shell Club, 408 North Sycamore Avenue, Los Angeles, California 90036, can send you information about a corresponding membership.

Sports Items/
Trading Cards

IT'S UP TO YOU

Baseball cards were first published in 1887, and baseball, football, basketball, hockey and soccer cards are still the biggest part of the *Sports Fan World*.

You can also specialize in collecting plaster statues and plastic dolls of the players—pennants, caps or shirts of the team—autographed balls for all sports, or autographed photographs of the players.

Game schedules are another collecting idea (they can be picked up at ballparks, banks, stores, sometimes at gas stations, or by writing to the teams).

WHERE TO LOOK

At garage sales, you'll often find a bonanza of sports cards that parents are trying to unload. Cards at swap meets will be more expensive (dealers know what they're worth), but you can still find some bargains. Trading cards can be found in packages of gum from grocery and candy stores. You can also buy cards in sets, from dealers of sports items. And by all means, trade with your friends.

Souvenir stands at ballgames are a good bet for pennants, caps, and other sports fan collectibles. Sometimes the ballpark or stadium itself will have special giveaways for fans when they arrive.

GETTING IT TOGETHER

Trading cards can be kept in shoe boxes or file boxes, but you'll really know what you have if you put them into the special plastic pages made to hold trading cards.

Then you can put these pages in three-ring notebook binders, grouped according to years or teams. The main idea is to keep the cards from being handled so that they won't get scratched, bent, or damaged in any way.

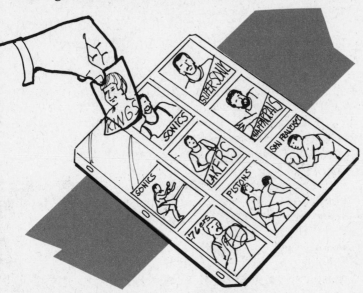

THE COLLECTOR'S DREAM

Keep your eyes open for cards made before the 1970s, and for the Kellogg's 3-D cards of 1971.

The most expensive baseball player card is the one with a picture of Honus Wagner on it. He was the star shortstop for the Pittsburgh Pirates many years ago. He forced a cigarette company to stop using his picture, and only 19 of these cards can be located today. Recently one sold for more than $3,000.

HELP! AND MORE HELP—

Sport Americana Alphabetical Baseball Card Checklist by Dr. J. Beckett and Dennis Eckes; P.O. Box 332, Bowling Green, Ohio 43402.

Stamps

IT'S UP TO YOU

Every country in the world issues postage stamps. They all have to be different. Almost all foreign countries have a time limit on the use of their stamps (from three to six months). Therefore, they are continually putting out new stamps. Because there are so many stamps made you can concentrate on collecting stamps picturing animals, birds, machines, sports, people, flowers, jobs, and stamps of one particular country, or practically any other subject you wish.

You might like to collect commemorative stamps issued for special events or anniversaries (like the Bicentennial stamps). There are stamps put out to honor a famous person (like the W. C. Fields stamp).

You might specialize in airmail stamps or precancelled stamps, which are sold only to the holder of a permit. They have had a cancellation imprinted on them *before* the sale, to make it easier to put through large amounts of mail.

Some people collect postage meter imprints. The design of the stamp is either printed on the envelope or on a gummed, printed sticker which is used *instead* of a stamp.

Very popular collectibles are first-day covers. These are envelopes printed especially for a special event and mailed on that day, usually from a place connected with the event. For example, first-day covers were mailed from Houston (the home of our NASA Mission Control

Manned Spacecraft Center) on the day when Armstrong walked on the moon.

WHERE TO LOOK

Save envelopes of letters received by your family. Make friends with business people in your neighborhood who get letters from overseas, and ask them to save the envelopes for you.

The U.S. Postal Service puts out stamp kits for beginning collectors.

You can buy packets of stamps from stamp dealers or write to the Philatelic Sales Branch, U.S. Postal Service, Washington, D.C. 20265. Ask them to send you their free Form 3300 for ordering stamps.

HOW TO START

Tear off the entire corner of each envelope, and soak a group of these envelope corners in cold water. When the stamps become loose, slide them off the paper and place the stamps face-down on a clean, dry sheet of paper. When they've completely dried, you can slip them into labeled envelopes or mount the stamps in stamp albums.

If you find that you have two copies of the same stamp, try to trade with a friend who has doubles of something you don't have.

GETTING IT TOGETHER

Handle your stamps with tweezers, because the skin of your hands has oils and acids which affect the gum, ink, and paper of the stamp. Besides, fingers can get stamps just plain dirty!

You can buy albums made especially to hold one particular type of stamp, or group of stamps. There are other stamp albums that are blank for you to use as you wish.

NEVER GLUE YOUR STAMPS ON THE PAGE.
Instead, use stamp hinges (see picture below).

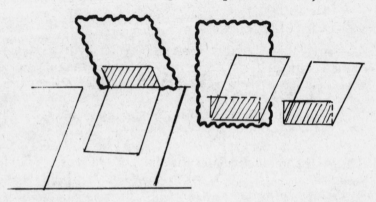

Most serious collectors arrange their stamps chronologically—based on the *year* when the stamp was first put out. Others group their stamps according to *country*.

GOOD TO KNOW

Certain countries have perforations (little rows of holes between the stamps) that are spaced and sized differently from others. If you know as much as possible about your stamps, you can, for example, measure the perforations with a perforation gauge to tell whether you have the real thing or a counterfeit!

Often a country will print postage for another country. For example, Liechtenstein is a very small country (only 28 people in their police force and no army). It has all of its stamps printed in Switzerland. The Jeffries Banknote Company in Los Angeles prints not only stamps but money as well for many other countries.

TALKING THE LANGUAGE

- Freaks — stamps with incorrect perforations, ink blots, shifted color, or other production accidents; not design errors.

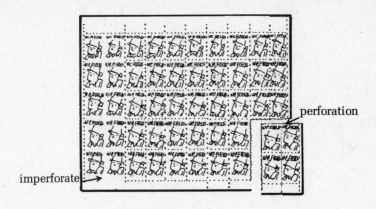

imperforate
perforation

- Imperforate—stamps without perforations.
- Margin—the border outside the printed area of a stamp or sheet of stamps.
- Perforation—the line of holes between stamps to make it easy to tear them apart.
- Philatelist—the fancy name for a stamp collector.
- Precancels—stamps with the cancellation printed on them before they are sold.

THE COLLECTOR'S DREAM

The most rare are stamps with printing errors. For example, when part of a design is turned upside down or one stamp of the wrong denomination shows up in the middle of a sheet. Learn about the various mistakes possible, and try to find one in newly issued stamps before anyone else does!

HELP! AND MORE HELP—

Stamp Collector, Van Dahl Publications, Box 10, Albany, Oregon 97321, is an excellent weekly newspaper full of articles, hints, columns and ads.

M. Meghrig & Sons, 329 Park Avenue South, New York, New York 10003 or 5352 Wilshire Boulevard, Los Angeles, California 90036, has a catalog that lists supplies as well as guides and stamps for sale.

Stickers

IT'S UP TO YOU

Kids went sticker crazy recently. As a result, lots of companies put out new stickers to fill the demand. You can collect any subject you wish in the world of printed paste-ons.

Some are gummed (you wet the back to stick them on). Others are self-adhesive (you peel off paper to get to the sticky surface in back).

Stickers come in a large variety of sizes and shapes, with pictures ranging from animals to witches. You can get them singly, in candy and gumwrap packages—or as complete sets (flags of the world, presidents of the United States and so on). There are 3-D stickers made from thick plastic and some with googly eyes that move. There are stickers with funny sayings, monsters, ads of all sorts, and even stickers that glow in the dark!

WHERE TO LOOK

Dime and stationery stores, giftshops, supermarkets, souvenir stands—almost any retail store can provide some kind of sticker. Often it's an ad for a product. For example, some oil companies put out stickers with their designs on 'em. Manufacturers give or sell them as special offers in cereal boxes. Companies sometimes tell about these special offers in advertisements in comic books.

Ask your friends and your folks. You'll probably find that the kitchen drawer has a neglected sticker or two of some sort.

And stickers are for trading—Trade, trade, trade, and fill in the gaps in your collection!

GETTING IT TOGETHER

Scrapbooks are the best way to keep stickers, especially

albums with the plastic pages to protect your collection. Do NOT permanently stick the stickers on the pages.

Some kids cover their school notebooks with their sticker collection. Whenever possible, keep them in their original packages.

HELP! AND MORE HELP—

Dennison Company, Consumer Products Division, Framingham, Massachusetts 01701. Write to them for a catalog of stickers.

Index